# THE Book Lover's JOURNAL

# THE Book Lover's JOURNAL

FELICITY FORSTER

This edition published in 2025 by Sirius Publishing, a division of
Arcturus Publishing Limited,
26/27 Bickels Yard, 151–153 Bermondsey Street,
London SE1 3HA



ISBN: 978-1-3988-5039-2
AD012440US

Printed in China

# CONTENTS

# INTRODUCTION

There's nothing like the feeling of getting lost in a good book, whether you're curled up on the sofa on a rainy day, passing the time while traveling on a busy train, lying on a beach on a summer holiday, or calming your mind before falling asleep every night. Discovering a new book can feel like finding a new friend.

## The joy of reading

I still remember the actual moment I "got it" when learning to read. It felt like a superpower—if I could read one book, I could read *all the books*! One of the best things about books is that they can take us on amazing journeys. They allow us to experience other lands, real or imagined, other times, and other people. They stimulate and energize our minds, making us think, feel, learn, laugh, cry, imagine, escape, empathize and discover. They help us to understand other minds, giving us direct access to writers' thoughts and experiences, from ancient times to the present day. They can also help us to look inward to reveal universal truths about the human condition.

A passion for books often starts in childhood or adolescence, and once we discover the joy of reading, it can become a lifelong obsession. You often hear people referring to themselves as "voracious" readers, or that they "devour" books. These sorts of terms show how passionate we can become about books and reading.

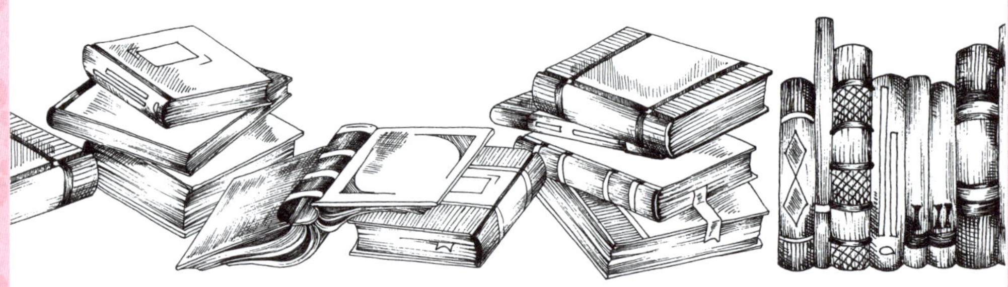

Many of us have a favorite book (or several) that we read more than once and treasure throughout our lives. We may feel a strong connection to the plot or characters, or enjoy going on the same journey again and again from the beginning, sometimes seeing things differently as we get older. A book may bring our own thoughts, dilemmas, and desires into focus, and sometimes it might even feel like a window into our soul.

Just as books can act as a mirror to our hopes and dreams, they can also expand our horizons and inspire us to change and grow. We can learn from other people's stories and see them as valuable sources of wisdom and insight. Books can have a huge influence on us as individuals and even on the entire world.

## Benefits of reading

As well as being a joyful activity in itself, reading has health and emotional benefits too. It is often said that *reading is to the mind what exercise is to the body*. Here are a few benefits of reading:

- Reduces stress
- Aids relaxation
- Improves concentration and memory
- Expands vocabulary, knowledge, and understanding
- Increases intelligence
- Enhances imagination and creativity
- Provides a positive distraction from negativity

Although reading is usually done as a solitary activity, it can also bring people together—you can join book clubs or get involved in discussion groups about books, whether in person or online.

## Printed books, ebooks or audiobooks?

Many people prefer reading printed books. Who doesn't love the smell of the pages (especially old library books!), the feeling of cracking open a new spine, and bookmarking your progress while watching the thickness of the remaining pages grow narrower? Printed books also look beautiful on our bookshelves, becoming much-loved objects and mementoes to revisit and treasure over the years.

But there are plenty of good reasons for reading ebooks and listening to audiobooks too. Going digital means all your books can be kept in one place, accessible wherever you go—you can effectively carry your entire collection in a small bag. You can also order an ebook or audiobook and start reading/listening immediately, without

## Genres

Fiction
Adventure stories
Classics
Comic books and graphic novels
Crime
Fairy tales, fables and folk tales
Fantasy
Historical fiction
Horror
Humour and satire
Literary fiction
Mystery
Poetry
Plays
Romance
Science fiction
Short stories
Thrillers
War
Women's fiction
Young adult
Nonfiction
Autobiography and memoir
Biography
Essays
History
Self-help

having to go to a book shop or library, or wait for delivery. Audiobooks have the additional advantage that they can be listened to while walking or driving, and many people believe they actually elevate the book beyond its text.

## How to use this journal

This journal has been specially designed for you to make a written record of your own personal reading journey, keeping all the information about the books you have read in one place. For each book, there are sections allowing you to rate how much you like the characters, plot, and writing style; write your own short summary of the book; jot down some memorable quotes; and make lists of other books by the same author. When recording each book's genre, it may help to refer to the list on page 8 opposite.

At the end of the journal you'll find space for making a list of the books you've read and reviewed, and just as importantly, a "TBR" list—books to be read. Overall, this journal will help you plan, track, and review your literary history, guide your thoughts while you're reading, and inspire your future reading choices. Happy reading!

*Felicity Forster*

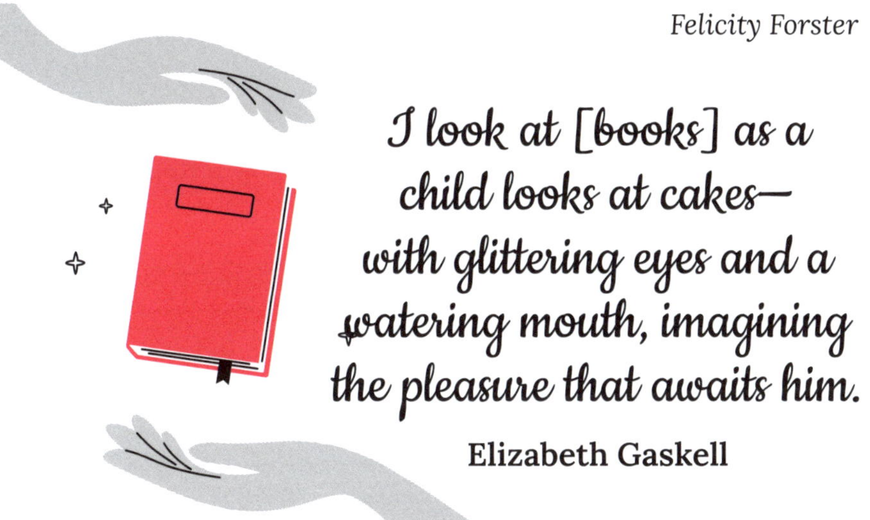

*I look at [books] as a child looks at cakes— with glittering eyes and a watering mouth, imagining the pleasure that awaits him.*

**Elizabeth Gaskell**

## Book title

..........................................................................................................

..........................................................................................................

Written by

..........................................................................................................

..........................................................................................................

Year of publication ..............................................................................

Number of pages ...................................................................................

Fiction ................................................ Nonfiction ....................................

Genre..........................................................................................................

..........................................................................................................

Date started.......................................... Completed......................................

| Characters | Plot | Writing | Overall rating |
| --- | --- | --- | --- |
| ☆☆☆☆☆ | ☆☆☆☆☆ | ☆☆☆☆☆ | ☆☆☆☆☆ |

How I discovered this book

..........................................................................................................

..........................................................................................................

..........................................................................................................

..........................................................................................................

..........................................................................................................

What the book is about

Book summary

*We read to know we're not alone.*

**William Nicholson**

Main characters

My favorite character was

Why I liked this character

Main themes

........................................

Writing style

........................................

Memorable quotes

........................................

........................................

........................................

........................................

........................................

........................................

........................................

........................................

........................................

........................................

........................................

........................................

........................................

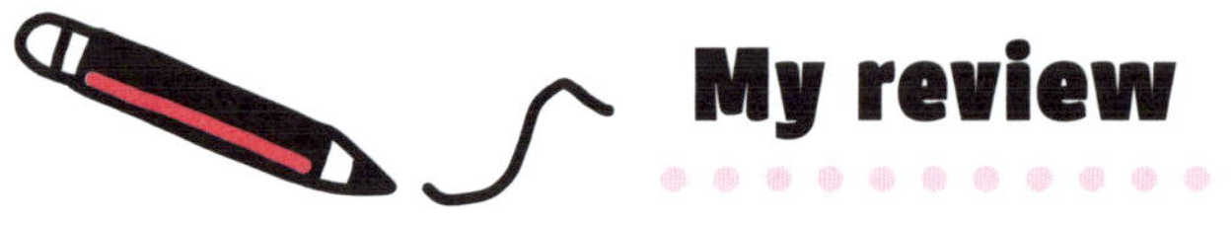

# My review

First impressions

Review

What I liked
most about the book

.........................................................................................

.........................................................................................

.........................................................................................

.........................................................................................

.........................................................................................

.........................................................................................

What I disliked

.........................................................................................

.........................................................................................

.........................................................................................

.........................................................................................

.........................................................................................

*You can never get a cup of tea large enough or a book long enough to suit me.*

C. S. Lewis

Other books in the same series

Other books by the same author

Other books with similar themes

# Book title

..................................................

..................................................

Written by

..................................................

..................................................

Year of publication ..................................................

Number of pages ..................................................

Fiction .................................. Nonfiction ..................................

Genre..................................................

..................................................

Date started .................................. Completed..................................

| Characters | Plot | Writing | Overall rating |
|---|---|---|---|
| ☆☆☆☆☆ | ☆☆☆☆☆ | ☆☆☆☆☆ | ☆☆☆☆☆ |

How I discovered this book

..................................................

..................................................

..................................................

..................................................

..................................................

What the book is about

Book summary

*If one cannot enjoy reading a book over and over again, there is no use in reading it at all.*

Oscar Wilde

Main characters

My favorite character was

Why I liked this character

Main themes

Writing style

Memorable quotes

# My review

First impressions

Review

What I liked most about the book

.......................................................................................................

.......................................................................................................

.......................................................................................................

.......................................................................................................

.......................................................................................................

.......................................................................................................

.......................................................................................................

What I disliked

.......................................................................................................

.......................................................................................................

.......................................................................................................

.......................................................................................................

*Sleep is good, he said, and books are better.*

**George R. R. Martin**

Other books in the same series

..........................................................................................................................................

..........................................................................................................................................

..........................................................................................................................................

..........................................................................................................................................

..........................................................................................................................................

..........................................................................................................................................

..........................................................................................................................................

..........................................................................................................................................

..........................................................................................................................................

..........................................................................................................................................

..........................................................................................................................................

Other books by the same author

..........................................................................................................................................

..........................................................................................................................................

..........................................................................................................................................

..........................................................................................................................................

..........................................................................................................................................

..........................................................................................................................................

..........................................................................................................................................

..........................................................................................................................................

..........................................................................................................................................

Other books with similar themes

## Book title

..............................................................................................................

..............................................................................................................

Written by

..............................................................................................................

..............................................................................................................

Year of publication ..............................................................................

Number of pages ................................................................................

Fiction ................................................ Nonfiction ...................................

Genre..........................................................................................................

..............................................................................................................

Date started ........................................ Completed.....................................

| Characters | Plot | Writing | Overall rating |
|---|---|---|---|
| ☆☆☆☆☆ | ☆☆☆☆☆ | ☆☆☆☆☆ | ☆☆☆☆☆ |

How I discovered this book

..............................................................................................................

..............................................................................................................

..............................................................................................................

..............................................................................................................

..............................................................................................................

What the book is about

Book summary

Books are a uniquely portable magic.

Stephen King

Main characters

.......................................................................................................................

.......................................................................................................................

.......................................................................................................................

.......................................................................................................................

.......................................................................................................................

My favorite character was

.......................................................................................................................

.......................................................................................................................

.......................................................................................................................

.......................................................................................................................

.......................................................................................................................

Why I liked this character

.......................................................................................................................

.......................................................................................................................

.......................................................................................................................

.......................................................................................................

...............................................................................................

.........................................................................................

.........................................................................................

.........................................................................................

Main themes

..........

Writing style

..........

Memorable quotes

..........

..........

..........

..........

..........

..........

..........

..........

..........

..........

..........

## My review

First impressions

Review

What I liked
most about the book

What I disliked

*Never trust anyone who has not brought a book with them.*

**Lemony Snicket**

Other books in the same series

Other books by the same author

Other books with similar themes

# Book title

..............................................................................................................

..............................................................................................................

Written by

..............................................................................................................

..............................................................................................................

Year of publication ..................................................................................

Number of pages .....................................................................................

Fiction ................................................. Nonfiction ......................................

Genre......................................................................................................

..............................................................................................................

Date started ........................................... Completed.......................................

| Characters | Plot | Writing | Overall rating |
|---|---|---|---|
| ☆☆☆☆☆ | ☆☆☆☆☆ | ☆☆☆☆☆ | ☆☆☆☆☆ |

How I discovered this book

..............................................................................................................

..............................................................................................................

..............................................................................................................

..............................................................................................................

..............................................................................................................

What the book is about

..................................................................................................

..................................................................................................

..................................................................................................

..................................................................................................

..................................................................................................

Book summary

..................................................................................................

..................................................................................................

..................................................................................................

..................................................................................................

..................................................................................................

..................................................................................................

..................................................................................................

..................................................................................................

..................................................................................................

..................................................................................................

..................................................................................................

*The more that you read, the more things you will know. The more that you learn, the more places you'll go.*

**Dr Seuss**

Main characters

.........................................................................................................

.........................................................................................................

.........................................................................................................

.........................................................................................................

.........................................................................................................

My favorite character was

.........................................................................................................

.........................................................................................................

.........................................................................................................

.........................................................................................................

.........................................................................................................

Why I liked this character

.........................................................................................................

.........................................................................................................

.........................................................................................................

.........................................................................................................

.........................................................................................................

.........................................................................................................

.........................................................................................................

.........................................................................................................

Main themes

Writing style

Memorable quotes

# My review

First impressions

Review

What I liked most about the book

..........................................................................................

..........................................................................................

..........................................................................................

..........................................................................................

..........................................................................................

..........................................................................................

What I disliked

..........................................................................................

..........................................................................................

..........................................................................................

..........................................................................................

..........................................................................................

..........................................................................................

*I find television very educating. Every time somebody turns on the set, I go into the other room and read a book.*

Groucho Marx

Other books in the same series

Other books by the same author

Other books with similar themes

## Book title

..............................................................................................................

..............................................................................................................

Written by

..............................................................................................................

..............................................................................................................

Year of publication ..........................................................................

Number of pages ..............................................................................

Fiction ................................................ Nonfiction ...................................

Genre......................................................................................................

..............................................................................................................

Date started ........................................ Completed ......................................

| Characters | Plot | Writing | Overall rating |
|---|---|---|---|
| ☆☆☆☆☆ | ☆☆☆☆☆ | ☆☆☆☆☆ | ☆☆☆☆☆ |

How I discovered this book

..............................................................................................................

..............................................................................................................

..............................................................................................................

..............................................................................................................

..............................................................................................................

What the book is about

..................................................................................................

..................................................................................................

..................................................................................................

..................................................................................................

..................................................................................................

Book summary

..................................................................................................

..................................................................................................

..................................................................................................

..................................................................................................

..................................................................................................

..................................................................................................

..................................................................................................

..................................................................................................

*I declare after all there is no enjoyment like reading! How much sooner one tires of any thing than of a book! When I have a house of my own, I shall be miserable if I have not an excellent library.*

**Jane Austen**

Main characters

My favorite character was

Why I liked this character

Main themes

Writing style

Memorable quotes

# My review

First impressions

Review

What I liked most about the book

..............................................................................................................

..............................................................................................................

..............................................................................................................

..............................................................................................................

..............................................................................................................

What I disliked

..............................................................................................................

..............................................................................................................

..............................................................................................................

..............................................................................................................

*Think before you speak.*
*Read before you think.*

**Fran Lebowitz**

Other books in the same series

...............................................................................................................................

...............................................................................................................................

...............................................................................................................................

...............................................................................................................................

...............................................................................................................................

...............................................................................................................................

...............................................................................................................................

...............................................................................................................................

...............................................................................................................................

...............................................................................................................................

...............................................................................................................................

Other books by the same author

...............................................................................................................................

...............................................................................................................................

...............................................................................................................................

...............................................................................................................................

...............................................................................................................................

...............................................................................................................................

...............................................................................................................................

...............................................................................................................................

...............................................................................................................................

Other books with similar themes

# Book title

..........................................................................................

..........................................................................................

Written by

..........................................................................................

..........................................................................................

Year of publication ..........................................................................

Number of pages ..............................................................................

Fiction .................................... Nonfiction ..................................

Genre.........................................................................................

..........................................................................................

Date started.................................. Completed....................................

| Characters | Plot | Writing | Overall rating |
|---|---|---|---|
| ☆☆☆☆☆ | ☆☆☆☆☆ | ☆☆☆☆☆ | ☆☆☆☆☆ |

How I discovered this book

..........................................................................................

..........................................................................................

..........................................................................................

..........................................................................................

..........................................................................................

What the book is about

Book summary

*Books are mirrors: you only see in them what you already have inside you.*

Carlos Ruiz Zafón

Main characters

My favorite character was

Why I liked this character

Main themes

..........

Writing style

..........

Memorable quotes

..........

..........

..........

..........

..........

..........

..........

..........

..........

..........

# My review

First impressions

Review

What I liked
most about the book

.......................................................................................

.......................................................................................

.......................................................................................

.......................................................................................

.......................................................................................

.......................................................................................

What I disliked

.......................................................................................

.......................................................................................

.......................................................................................

.......................................................................................

.......................................................................................

*In the case of good books, the point is not to see how many of them you can get through, but rather how many can get through to you.*

Mortimer J. Adler

Other books in the same series

Other books by the same author

Other books with similar themes

# Book title

..........................................................................................

..........................................................................................

Written by

..........................................................................................

..........................................................................................

Year of publication ..........................................................................

Number of pages ..............................................................................

Fiction ........................................ Nonfiction ..................................

Genre..........................................................................................

..........................................................................................

Date started.................................. Completed...................................

| Characters | Plot | Writing | Overall rating |
|---|---|---|---|
| ☆☆☆☆☆ | ☆☆☆☆☆ | ☆☆☆☆☆ | ☆☆☆☆☆ |

How I discovered this book

..........................................................................................

..........................................................................................

..........................................................................................

..........................................................................................

..........................................................................................

What the book is about

Book summary

*Words can be like X-rays if you use them properly—they'll go through anything. You read and you're pierced.*

**Aldous Huxley**

Main characters

My favorite character was

Why I liked this character

Main themes

Writing style

Memorable quotes

# My review

First impressions

Review

What I liked most about the book

........................................................................................................................

........................................................................................................................

........................................................................................................................

........................................................................................................................

........................................................................................................................

What I disliked

........................................................................................................................

........................................................................................................................

........................................................................................................................

........................................................................................................................

........................................................................................................................

........................................................................................................................

*We live for books.*

**Umberto Eco**

Other books in the same series

Other books by the same author

Other books with similar themes

# Book title

........................................................................................................

........................................................................................................

Written by

........................................................................................................

........................................................................................................

Year of publication ..............................................................................

Number of pages ..................................................................................

Fiction ............................................. Nonfiction ....................................

Genre.....................................................................................................

........................................................................................................

Date started ......................................... Completed .....................................

| Characters | Plot | Writing | Overall rating |
|---|---|---|---|
| ☆☆☆☆☆ | ☆☆☆☆☆ | ☆☆☆☆☆ | ☆☆☆☆☆ |

How I discovered this book

........................................................................................................

........................................................................................................

........................................................................................................

........................................................................................................

........................................................................................................

What the book is about

..........................................................................................................

..........................................................................................................

..........................................................................................................

..........................................................................................................

..........................................................................................................

Book summary

..........................................................................................................

..........................................................................................................

..........................................................................................................

..........................................................................................................

..........................................................................................................

..........................................................................................................

..........................................................................................................

..........................................................................................................

..........................................................................................................

*Books are the plane, and the train, and the road. They are the destination, and the journey. They are home.*

**Anna Quindlen**

Main characters

My favorite character was

Why I liked this character

Main themes

..................................................

Writing style

..................................................

Memorable quotes

..................................................

..................................................

..................................................

..................................................

..................................................

..................................................

..................................................

..................................................

..................................................

..................................................

# My review

First impressions

Review

What I liked most about the book

..........................................................................................

..........................................................................................

..........................................................................................

..........................................................................................

..........................................................................................

..........................................................................................

What I disliked

..........................................................................................

..........................................................................................

..........................................................................................

..........................................................................................

..........................................................................................

*A classic is a book that has never finished saying what it has to say.*

**Italo Calvino**

Other books in the same series

Other books by the same author

Other books with similar themes

# Book title

........................................................................................................

........................................................................................................

Written by

........................................................................................................

........................................................................................................

Year of publication ...............................................................................

Number of pages ...................................................................................

Fiction ........................................................ Nonfiction ...................................

Genre.......................................................................................................

........................................................................................................

Date started............................................... Completed......................................

| Characters | Plot | Writing | Overall rating |
|---|---|---|---|
| ☆☆☆☆☆ | ☆☆☆☆☆ | ☆☆☆☆☆ | ☆☆☆☆☆ |

How I discovered this book

........................................................................................................

........................................................................................................

........................................................................................................

........................................................................................................

........................................................................................................

What the book is about

..........................................................................................................................................

..........................................................................................................................................

..........................................................................................................................................

..........................................................................................................................................

..........................................................................................................................................

Book summary

..........................................................................................................................................

..........................................................................................................................................

..........................................................................................................................................

..........................................................................................................................................

..........................................................................................................................................

..........................................................................................................................................

..........................................................................................................................................

*Reading is escape, and the opposite of escape; it's a way to make contact with reality after a day of making things up, and it's a way of making contact with someone else's imagination after a day that's all too real.*

**Nora Ephron**

Main characters

My favorite character was

Why I liked this character

Main themes

..........

Writing style

..........

Memorable quotes

..........

..........

..........

..........

..........

..........

..........

..........

..........

## My review

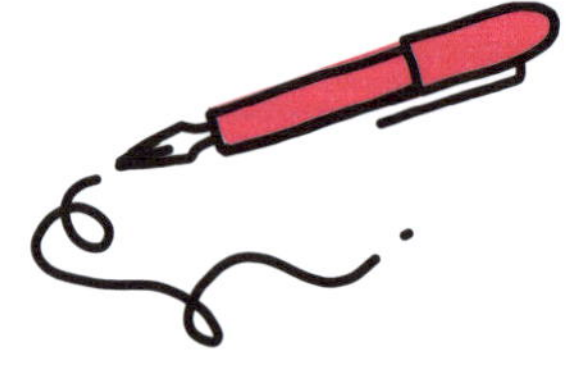

First impressions

Review

What I liked
most about the book

........................................................................................................

........................................................................................................

........................................................................................................

........................................................................................................

........................................................................................................

........................................................................................................

What I disliked

........................................................................................................

........................................................................................................

........................................................................................................

........................................................................................................

........................................................................................................

*The best books . . . are those that tell you what you know already.*

**George Orwell**

Other books in the same series

Other books by the same author

Other books with similar themes

# Book title

........................................................................................................................

........................................................................................................................

Written by

........................................................................................................................

........................................................................................................................

Year of publication ................................................................................

Number of pages ......................................................................................

Fiction ................................................ Nonfiction ..................................

Genre.......................................................................................................

........................................................................................................................

Date started............................................ Completed...................................

| Characters | Plot | Writing | Overall rating |
|---|---|---|---|
| ☆☆☆☆☆ | ☆☆☆☆☆ | ☆☆☆☆☆ | ☆☆☆☆☆ |

How I discovered this book

........................................................................................................................

........................................................................................................................

........................................................................................................................

........................................................................................................................

........................................................................................................................

What the book is about

Book summary

*If you don't like to read, you haven't found the right book.*

J. K. Rowling

Main characters

My favorite character was

Why I liked this character

Main themes

Writing style

Memorable quotes

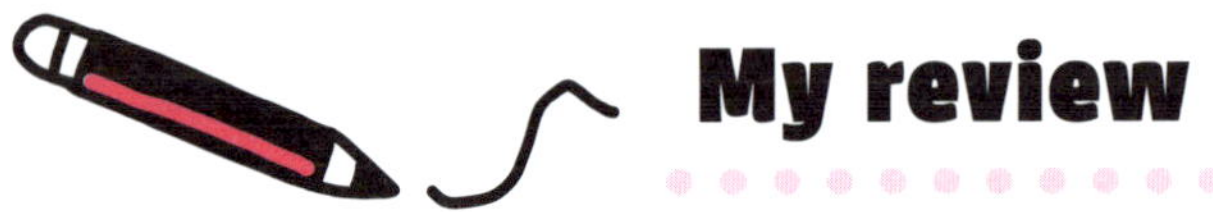

# My review

First impressions

Review

What I liked most about the book

..................................................

..................................................

..................................................

..................................................

..................................................

..................................................

What I disliked

..................................................

..................................................

..................................................

..................................................

*Today a reader, tomorrow a leader.*

**Margaret Fuller**

Other books in the same series

Other books by the same author

Other books with similar themes

# Book title

........................................................................................................

........................................................................................................

Written by

........................................................................................................

........................................................................................................

Year of publication ........................................................................

Number of pages ...........................................................................

Fiction ................................................ Nonfiction ................................

Genre...........................................................................................

........................................................................................................

Date started ....................................... Completed.................................

| Characters | Plot | Writing | Overall rating |
|---|---|---|---|
| ☆☆☆☆☆ | ☆☆☆☆☆ | ☆☆☆☆☆ | ☆☆☆☆☆ |

How I discovered this book

........................................................................................................

........................................................................................................

........................................................................................................

........................................................................................................

........................................................................................................

What the book is about

..........................................................................................................

..........................................................................................................

..........................................................................................................

..........................................................................................................

..........................................................................................................

Book summary

..........................................................................................................

..........................................................................................................

..........................................................................................................

..........................................................................................................

..........................................................................................................

..........................................................................................................

..............................................................

...........................................................

..........................................................

.....................................................

...................................................

...................................................

.....................................................

.......................................................

...........................................................

*Books should go where they will be most appreciated, and not sit unread, gathering dust on a forgotten shelf, don't you agree?*

**Christopher Paolini**

Main characters

My favorite character was

Why I liked this character

Main themes

........................................................................................................................................

Writing style

........................................................................................................................................

Memorable quotes

........................................................................................................................................

........................................................................................................................................

........................................................................................................................................

........................................................................................................................................

........................................................................................................................................

........................................................................................................................................

........................................................................................................................................

........................................................................................................................................

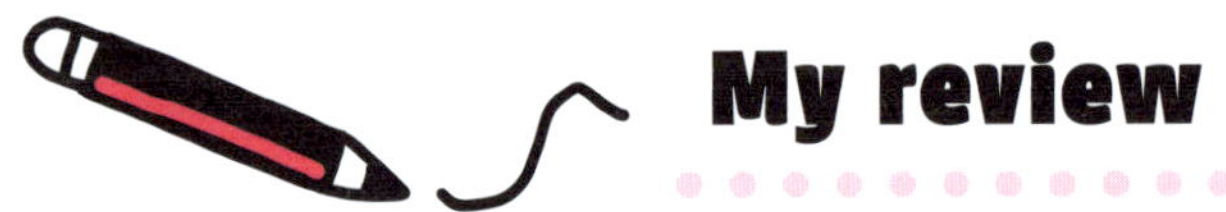

# My review

First impressions

Review

What I liked most about the book

..............................................................................................

..............................................................................................

..............................................................................................

..............................................................................................

..............................................................................................

..............................................................................................

What I disliked

..............................................................................................

..............................................................................................

..............................................................................................

..............................................................................................

*She read books as one would breathe air, to fill up and live.*

**Annie Dillard**

Other books in the same series

Other books by the same author

Other books with similar themes

# Book title

..........................................................................................................................................

..........................................................................................................................................

Written by

..........................................................................................................................................

..........................................................................................................................................

Year of publication ....................................................................................................

Number of pages .........................................................................................................

Fiction ......................................................... Nonfiction ..........................................

Genre .............................................................................................................................

..........................................................................................................................................

Date started ................................................ Completed ..........................................

| Characters | Plot | Writing | Overall rating |
|---|---|---|---|
| ☆☆☆☆☆ | ☆☆☆☆☆ | ☆☆☆☆☆ | ☆☆☆☆☆ |

How I discovered this book

..........................................................................................................................................

..........................................................................................................................................

..........................................................................................................................................

..........................................................................................................................................

..........................................................................................................................................

What the book is about

Book summary

People can lose their lives in libraries. They ought to be warned.

Saul Bellow

Main characters

My favorite character was

Why I liked this character

Main themes

..........

Writing style

..........

Memorable quotes

..........

..........

..........

..........

..........

..........

..........

..........

# My review

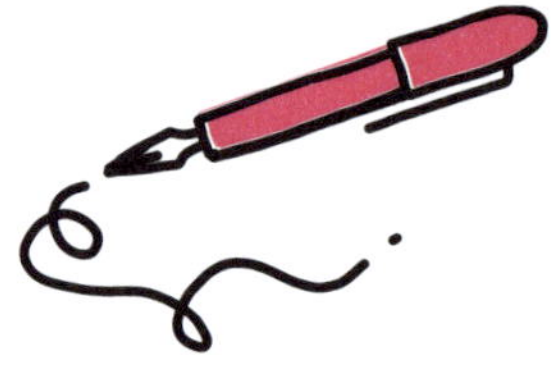

First impressions

Review

What I liked most about the book

........................................................................................

........................................................................................

........................................................................................

........................................................................................

........................................................................................

........................................................................................

What I disliked

........................................................................................

........................................................................................

........................................................................................

........................................................................................

........................................................................................

*A half-read book is a half-finished love affair.*

**David Mitchell**

Other books in the same series

Other books by the same author

Other books with similar themes

# Book title

..........................................................................................

..........................................................................................

Written by

..........................................................................................

..........................................................................................

Year of publication ..........................................................................

Number of pages ..............................................................................

Fiction .................................................... Nonfiction ..................................

Genre..........................................................................................

..........................................................................................

Date started.............................................. Completed.................................

| Characters | Plot | Writing | Overall rating |
|---|---|---|---|
| ☆☆☆☆☆ | ☆☆☆☆☆ | ☆☆☆☆☆ | ☆☆☆☆☆ |

How I discovered this book

..........................................................................................

..........................................................................................

..........................................................................................

..........................................................................................

..........................................................................................

What the book is about

Book summary

*A word after a word after a word is power.*

**Margaret Atwood**

Main characters

..........

..........

..........

..........

..........

My favorite character was

..........

..........

..........

..........

..........

Why I liked this character

..........

..........

..........

..........

..........

..........

..........

..........

Main themes

Writing style

Memorable quotes

# My review

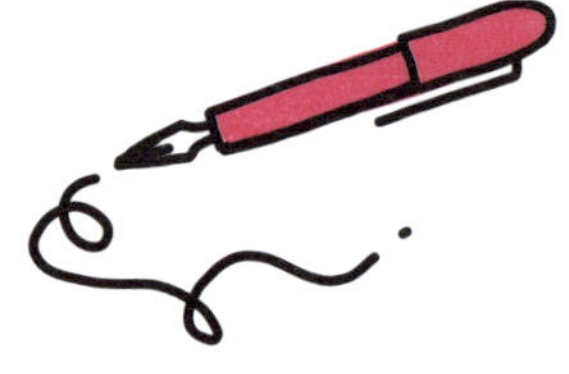

First impressions

Review

What I liked most about the book

.................................................................................................

.................................................................................................

.................................................................................................

.................................................................................................

.................................................................................................

.................................................................................................

What I disliked

.................................................................................................

.................................................................................................

.................................................................................................

.................................................................................................

*Reading brings us unknown friends.*

Honoré de Balzac

Other books in the same series

Other books by the same author

Other books with similar themes

# Book title

..........................................................................................................................

..........................................................................................................................

Written by

..........................................................................................................................

..........................................................................................................................

Year of publication ..............................................................................................

Number of pages ..................................................................................................

Fiction ........................................................ Nonfiction ......................................

Genre..........................................................................................................................

..........................................................................................................................

Date started................................................. Completed.......................................

| Characters | Plot | Writing | Overall rating |
|---|---|---|---|
| ☆☆☆☆☆ | ☆☆☆☆☆ | ☆☆☆☆☆ | ☆☆☆☆☆ |

How I discovered this book

..........................................................................................................................

..........................................................................................................................

..........................................................................................................................

..........................................................................................................................

..........................................................................................................................

What the book is about

Book summary

*Reading is the sole means by which we slip, involuntarily, often helplessly, into another's skin, another's voice, another's soul.*

**Joyce Carol Oates**

Main characters

My favorite character was

Why I liked this character

Main themes

..................................................................................................................................

Writing style

..................................................................................................................................

Memorable quotes

..................................................................................................................................

..................................................................................................................................

..................................................................................................................................

..................................................................................................................................

..................................................................................................................................

..................................................................................................................................

..................................................................................................................................

..................................................................................................................................

..................................................................................................................................

..................................................................................................................................

..................................................................................................................................

# My review

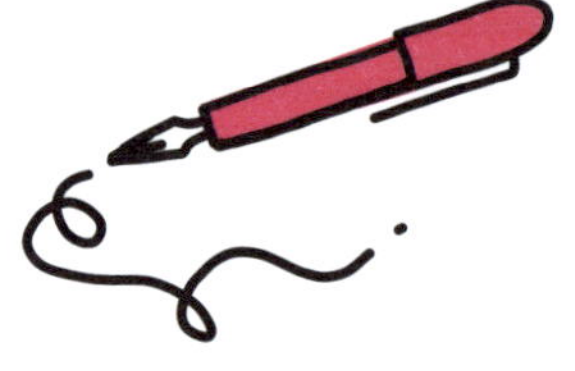

First impressions

Review

What I liked most about the book

........................................................................................................

........................................................................................................

........................................................................................................

........................................................................................................

........................................................................................................

........................................................................................................

What I disliked

........................................................................................................

........................................................................................................

........................................................................................................

........................................................................................................

*I kept always two books in my pocket, one to read, one to write in.*

**Robert Louis Stevenson**

Other books in the same series

Other books by the same author

Other books with similar themes

# Book title

.......................................................................................................

.......................................................................................................

Written by

.......................................................................................................

.......................................................................................................

Year of publication ......................................................................

Number of pages ...........................................................................

Fiction ........................................... Nonfiction ..............................

Genre..................................................................................................

.......................................................................................................

Date started ..................................... Completed...............................

| Characters | Plot | Writing | Overall rating |
|---|---|---|---|
| ☆☆☆☆☆ | ☆☆☆☆☆ | ☆☆☆☆☆ | ☆☆☆☆☆ |

How I discovered this book

.......................................................................................................

.......................................................................................................

.......................................................................................................

.......................................................................................................

.......................................................................................................

What the book is about

Book summary

*Books are no more threatened by Kindle than stairs by elevators.*

**Stephen Fry**

Main characters

..........................................................................................................................

..........................................................................................................................

..........................................................................................................................

..........................................................................................................................

..........................................................................................................................

My favorite character was

..........................................................................................................................

..........................................................................................................................

..........................................................................................................................

..........................................................................................................................

..........................................................................................................................

Why I liked this character

..........................................................................................................................

..........................................................................................................................

..........................................................................................................................

..........................................................................................................................

..........................................................................................................................

..........................................................................................................................

..........................................................................................................................

..........................................................................................................................

Main themes

................................................................................

Writing style

................................................................................

Memorable quotes

................................................................................

................................................................................

................................................................................

................................................................................

................................................................................

................................................................................

................................................................................

................................................................................

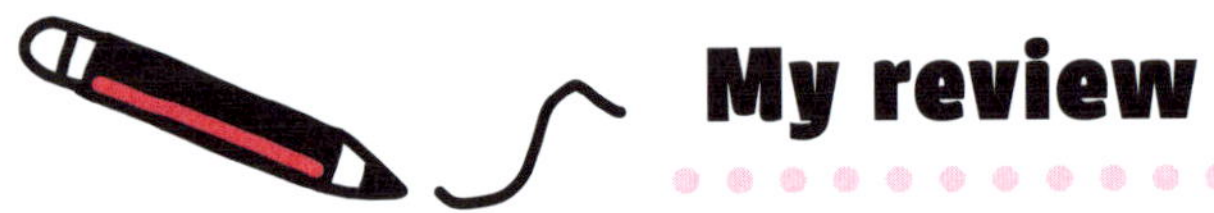

## My review

First impressions

Review

What I liked most about the book

.................................................................................................

.................................................................................................

.................................................................................................

.................................................................................................

.................................................................................................

.................................................................................................

What I disliked

.................................................................................................

.................................................................................................

.................................................................................................

.................................................................................................

.................................................................................................

.................................................................................................

*One glance at a book and you hear the voice of another person, perhaps someone dead for 1,000 years. To read is to voyage through time.*

**Carl Sagan**

Other books in the same series

Other books by the same author

Other books with similar themes

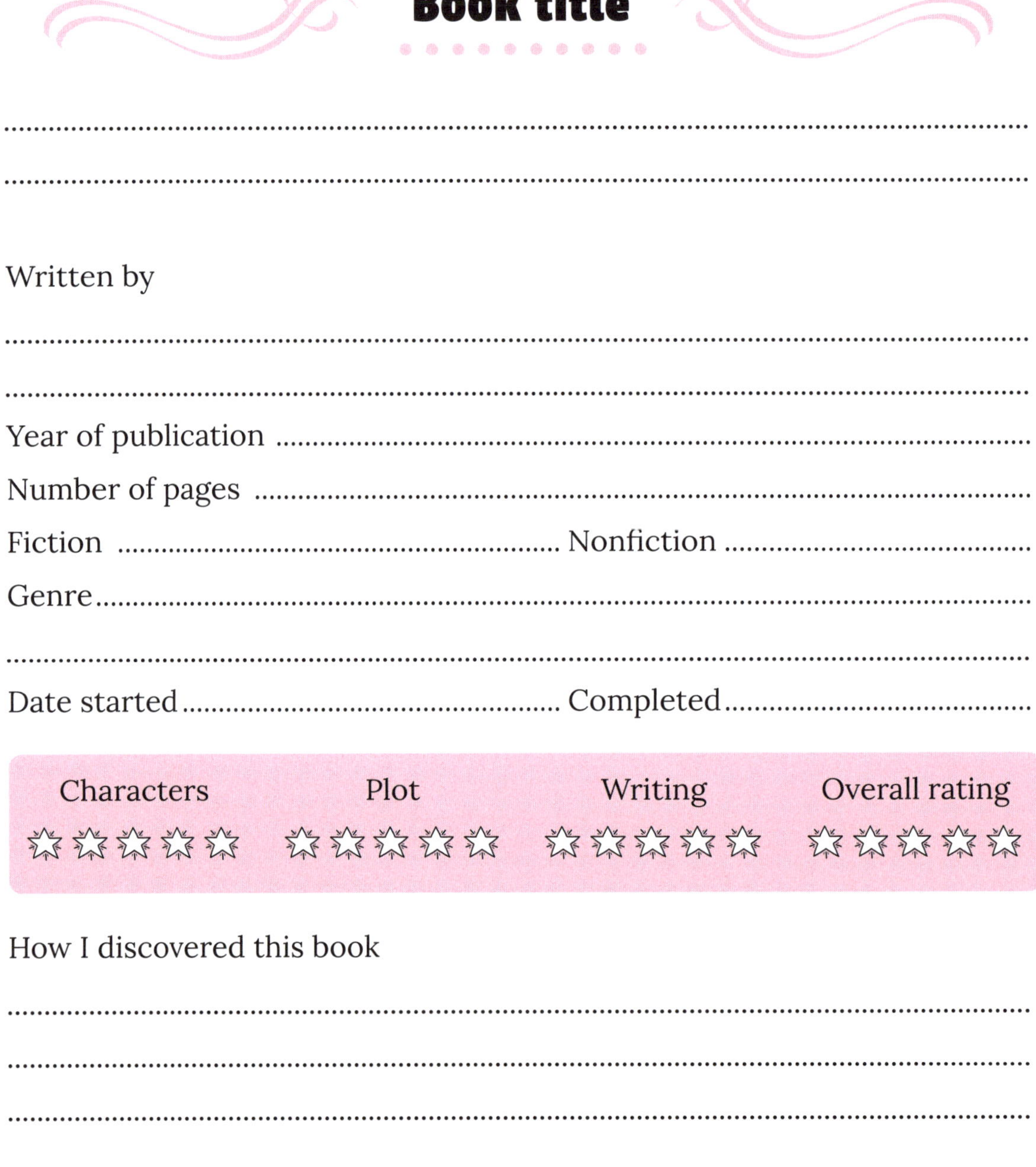

# Book title

..................................................................................................

..................................................................................................

Written by

..................................................................................................

..................................................................................................

Year of publication ..................................................................................

Number of pages .....................................................................................

Fiction ............................................... Nonfiction ...................................

Genre.......................................................................................................

..................................................................................................

Date started........................................ Completed..................................

| Characters | Plot | Writing | Overall rating |
|---|---|---|---|
| ☆☆☆☆☆ | ☆☆☆☆☆ | ☆☆☆☆☆ | ☆☆☆☆☆ |

How I discovered this book

..................................................................................................

..................................................................................................

..................................................................................................

..................................................................................................

..................................................................................................

What the book is about

Book summary

*Everything in the world exists in order to end up as a book.*

**Stéphane Mallarmé**

Main characters

My favorite character was

Why I liked this character

Main themes

..........................................................................................................

Writing style

..........................................................................................................

Memorable quotes

..........................................................................................................

..........................................................................................................

..........................................................................................................

..........................................................................................................

..........................................................................................................

..........................................................................................................

..........................................................................................................

..........................................................................................................

..........................................................................

..................................................

.................................................

................................................

...........................

# My review

First impressions

Review

What I liked most about the book

........................................................................................................................

........................................................................................................................

........................................................................................................................

........................................................................................................................

........................................................................................................................

........................................................................................................................

What I disliked

........................................................................................................................

........................................................................................................................

........................................................................................................................

........................................................................................................................

........................................................................................................................

........................................................................................................................

*A peasant that reads is a prince in waiting.*

**Walter Mosley**

Other books in the same series

Other books by the same author

Other books with similar themes

# Book title

..............................................................................................................

..............................................................................................................

Written by

..............................................................................................................

..............................................................................................................

Year of publication ..........................................................................

Number of pages ..............................................................................

Fiction ........................................... Nonfiction ...................................

Genre ..............................................................................................

..............................................................................................................

Date started ..................................... Completed ....................................

| Characters | Plot | Writing | Overall rating |
| --- | --- | --- | --- |
| ☆☆☆☆☆ | ☆☆☆☆☆ | ☆☆☆☆☆ | ☆☆☆☆☆ |

How I discovered this book

..............................................................................................................

..............................................................................................................

..............................................................................................................

..............................................................................................................

..............................................................................................................

What the book is about

Book summary

*A good bookshop is just a genteel Black Hole that knows how to read.*

**Terry Pratchett**

Main characters

My favorite character was

Why I liked this character

Main themes

Writing style

Memorable quotes

# My review

First impressions

Review

What I liked most about the book

........................................................................................................

........................................................................................................

........................................................................................................

........................................................................................................

........................................................................................................

........................................................................................................

........................................................................................................

What I disliked

........................................................................................................

........................................................................................................

........................................................................................................

........................................................................................................

........................................................................................................

........................................................................................................

........................................................................................................

*Show me a family of readers, and I will show you the people who move the world.*

**Napoleon Bonaparte**

Other books in the same series

Other books by the same author

Other books with similar themes

# Book title

..........................................................................................

..........................................................................................

Written by

..........................................................................................

..........................................................................................

Year of publication ..........................................................................

Number of pages ..............................................................................

Fiction ...................................................... Nonfiction ..............................................

Genre..............................................................................................

..........................................................................................

Date started................................................ Completed..............................................

| Characters | Plot | Writing | Overall rating |
|---|---|---|---|
| ☆☆☆☆☆ | ☆☆☆☆☆ | ☆☆☆☆☆ | ☆☆☆☆☆ |

How I discovered this book

..........................................................................................

..........................................................................................

..........................................................................................

..........................................................................................

..........................................................................................

What the book is about

Book summary

*I guess there are never enough books.*

**John Steinbeck**

Main characters

My favorite character was

Why I liked this character

Main themes

..........

Writing style

..........

Memorable quotes

..........

..........

..........

..........

..........

..........

..........

..........

..........

..........

..........

..........

# My review

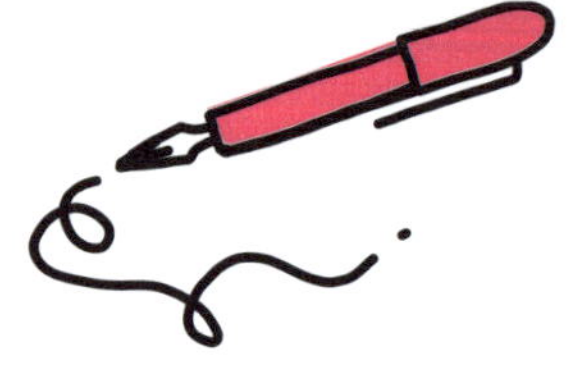

First impressions

Review

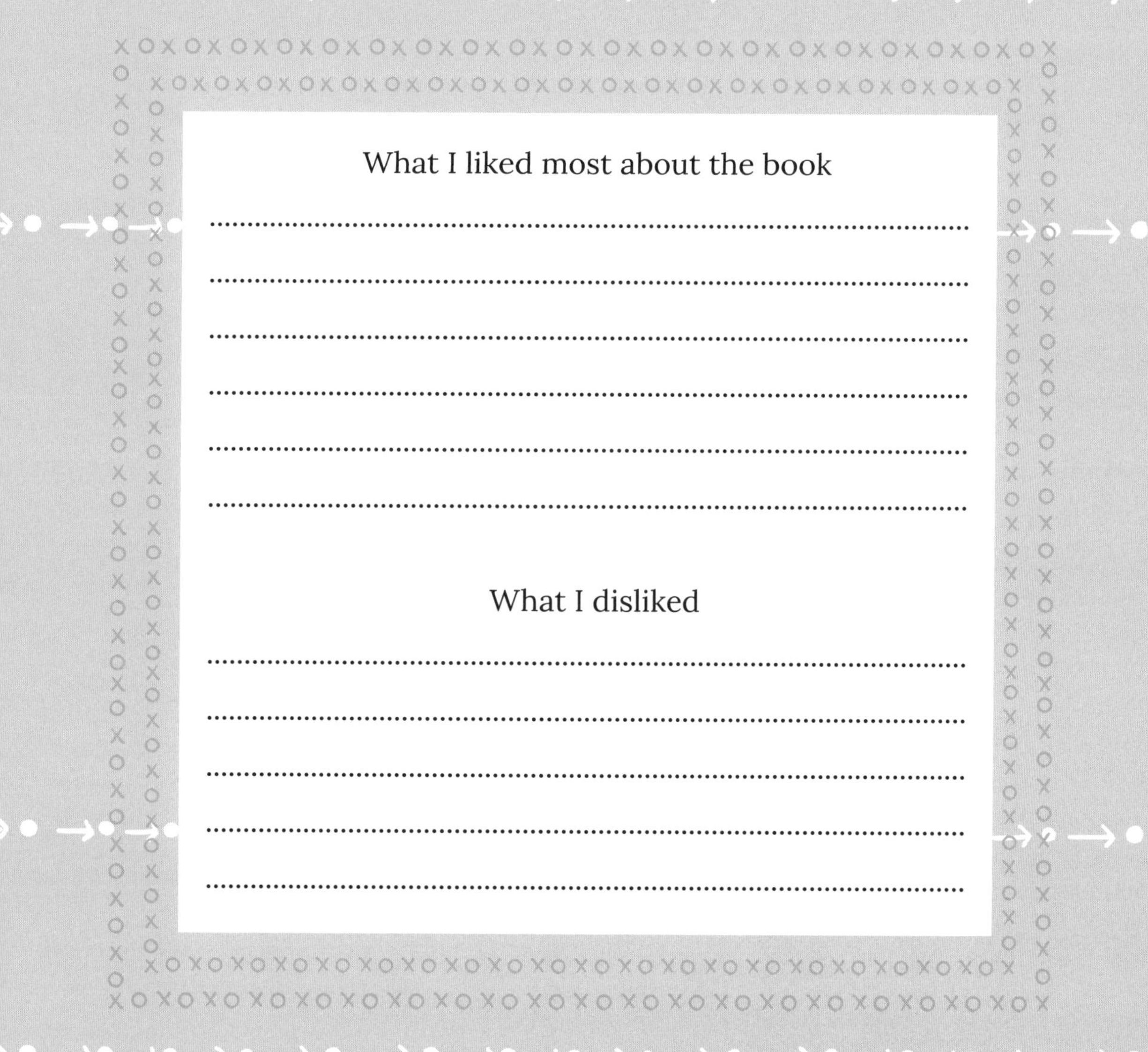


*To learn to read is to light a fire; every syllable that is spelled out is a spark.*

**Victor Hugo**

Other books in the same series

Other books by the same author

Other books with similar themes

# Book title

..........................................................................................

..........................................................................................

Written by

..........................................................................................

..........................................................................................

Year of publication ..........................................................................

Number of pages ..............................................................................

Fiction ........................................................ Nonfiction ...........................

Genre..............................................................................................

..........................................................................................

Date started.................................................. Completed...........................

| Characters | Plot | Writing | Overall rating |
| --- | --- | --- | --- |
| ☆☆☆☆☆ | ☆☆☆☆☆ | ☆☆☆☆☆ | ☆☆☆☆☆ |

How I discovered this book

..........................................................................................

..........................................................................................

..........................................................................................

..........................................................................................

..........................................................................................

What the book is about

..............................................................................................................

..............................................................................................................

..............................................................................................................

..............................................................................................................

..............................................................................................................

Book summary

..............................................................................................................

..............................................................................................................

..............................................................................................................

..............................................................................................................

..............................................................................................................

..............................................................................................................

..............................................................................................................

*When I look back, I am so impressed again with the life-giving power of literature. If I were a young person today, trying to gain a sense of myself in the world, I would do that again by reading, just as I did when I was young.*

**Maya Angelou**

Main characters

My favorite character was

Why I liked this character

Main themes

Writing style

Memorable quotes

## My review

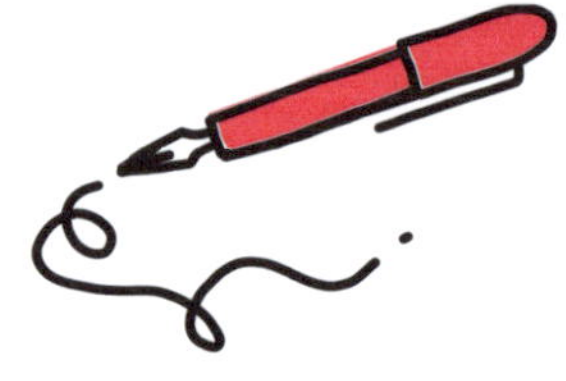

First impressions

Review

What I liked most about the book

........................................................................................................

........................................................................................................

........................................................................................................

........................................................................................................

........................................................................................................

........................................................................................................

........................................................................................................

What I disliked

........................................................................................................

........................................................................................................

........................................................................................................

........................................................................................................

*I am reading six books at once, the only way of reading; since, as you will agree, one book is only a single unaccompanied note, and to get the full sound, one needs ten others at the same time.*

**Virginia Woolf**

Other books in the same series

Other books by the same author

Other books with similar themes

# Book title

Written by

Year of publication

Number of pages

Fiction Nonfiction

Genre

Date started Completed

| Characters | Plot | Writing | Overall rating |
|---|---|---|---|
| ☆☆☆☆☆ | ☆☆☆☆☆ | ☆☆☆☆☆ | ☆☆☆☆☆ |

How I discovered this book

What the book is about

Book summary

*The reading of all good books is like conversation with the finest men of past centuries.*

René Descartes

Main characters

..........

..........

..........

..........

..........

My favorite character was

..........

..........

..........

..........

..........

Why I liked this character

..........

..........

..........

..........

..........

..........

..........

..........

Main themes

........................................................................................................................

Writing style

........................................................................................................................

Memorable quotes

........................................................................................................................

........................................................................................................................

........................................................................................................................

........................................................................................................................

........................................................................................................................

........................................................................................................................

........................................................................................................................

...............................................................................................................

.............................................................................................

...........................................

..........................................

........................................

............................

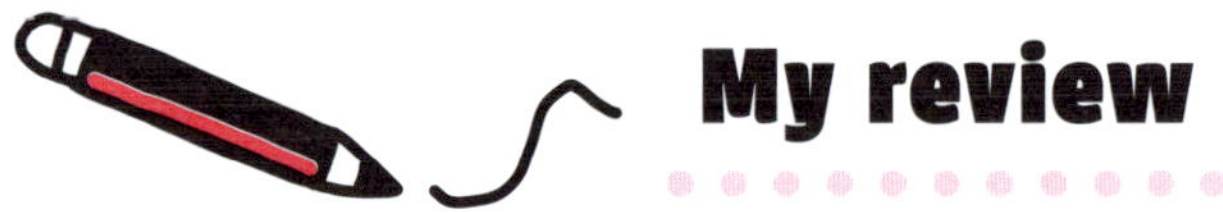

# My review

First impressions

Review

What I liked
most about the book

........................................................................................................

........................................................................................................

........................................................................................................

........................................................................................................

What I disliked

........................................................................................................

........................................................................................................

........................................................................................................

........................................................................................................

........................................................................................................

*So many books, so little time.*

**Frank Zappa**

Other books in the same series

Other books by the same author

Other books with similar themes

## Book title

........................................................................................................................

........................................................................................................................

Written by

........................................................................................................................

........................................................................................................................

Year of publication ...........................................................................................

Number of pages ................................................................................................

Fiction ................................................................. Nonfiction ........................................

Genre..................................................................................................................

........................................................................................................................

Date started.......................................................... Completed.......................................

| Characters | Plot | Writing | Overall rating |
|---|---|---|---|
| ☆☆☆☆☆ | ☆☆☆☆☆ | ☆☆☆☆☆ | ☆☆☆☆☆ |

How I discovered this book

........................................................................................................................

........................................................................................................................

........................................................................................................................

........................................................................................................................

........................................................................................................................

What the book is about

..........

..........

..........

..........

..........

Book summary

..........

..........

..........

..........

..........

..........

..........

..........

..........

*Libraries will get you through times of no money better than money will get you through times of no libraries.*

Anne Herbert

Main characters

My favorite character was

Why I liked this character

Main themes

Writing style

Memorable quotes

# My review

First impressions

Review

What I liked most about the book

................................................................................

................................................................................

................................................................................

................................................................................

................................................................................

................................................................................

What I disliked

................................................................................

................................................................................

................................................................................

................................................................................

................................................................................

*Only a generation of readers will spawn a generation of writers.*

**Steven Spielberg**

Other books in the same series

Other books by the same author

Other books with similar themes

# Book title

..................................................................................................................

..................................................................................................................

Written by

..................................................................................................................

..................................................................................................................

Year of publication ..........................................................................................

Number of pages ..............................................................................................

Fiction ........................................................... Nonfiction ..........................................

Genre.................................................................................................................

..................................................................................................................

Date started................................................. Completed..........................................

| Characters | Plot | Writing | Overall rating |
|---|---|---|---|
| ☆☆☆☆☆ | ☆☆☆☆☆ | ☆☆☆☆☆ | ☆☆☆☆☆ |

How I discovered this book

..................................................................................................................

..................................................................................................................

..................................................................................................................

..................................................................................................................

..................................................................................................................

What the book is about

Book summary

*Reading is to the mind what exercise is to the body.*

**Joseph Addison**

Main characters

My favorite character was

Why I liked this character

Main themes

..................................................................................................................................

Writing style

..................................................................................................................................

Memorable quotes

..................................................................................................................................

..................................................................................................................................

..................................................................................................................................

..................................................................................................................................

..................................................................................................................................

..................................................................................................................................

..................................................................................................................................

..................................................................................................................................

...........................................................................

........................................................................

......................................................................

...................................................................

..............................................

.....................................

..................................

....................................

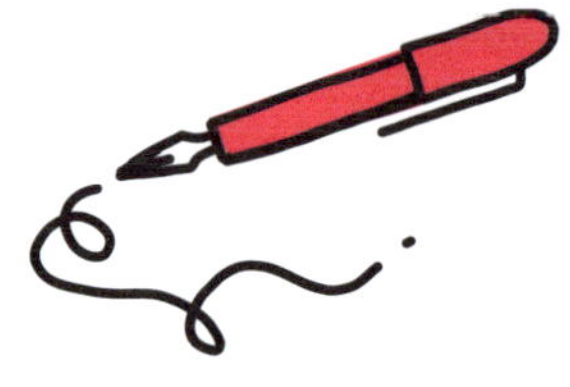

First impressions

Review

What I liked most about the book

What I disliked

*I couldn't live a week without a private library – indeed, I'd part with all my furniture and squat and sleep on the floor before I'd let go of the 1500 or so books I possess.*

H. P. Lovecraft

Other books in the same series

Other books by the same author

Other books with similar themes

# Book title

........................................................................................................

........................................................................................................

Written by

........................................................................................................

........................................................................................................

Year of publication ........................................................................

Number of pages ............................................................................

Fiction ..................................................... Nonfiction ....................................

Genre..............................................................................................

........................................................................................................

Date started ............................................. Completed ....................................

| Characters | Plot | Writing | Overall rating |
|---|---|---|---|
| ☆☆☆☆☆ | ☆☆☆☆☆ | ☆☆☆☆☆ | ☆☆☆☆☆ |

How I discovered this book

........................................................................................................

........................................................................................................

........................................................................................................

........................................................................................................

........................................................................................................

What the book is about

Book summary

No two persons ever read the same book.

Edmund Wilson

Main characters

..................................................................................................................................

..................................................................................................................................

..................................................................................................................................

..................................................................................................................................

..................................................................................................................................

My favorite character was

..................................................................................................................................

..................................................................................................................................

..................................................................................................................................

..................................................................................................................................

..................................................................................................................................

Why I liked this character

..................................................................................................................................

..................................................................................................................................

..................................................................................................................................

..............................................................................................

..................................................................................

...............................................................................

..............................................................................

.............................................................................

Main themes

..............................................................................................................

Writing style

..............................................................................................................

Memorable quotes

..............................................................................................................

..............................................................................................................

..............................................................................................................

..............................................................................................................

..............................................................................................................

..............................................................................................................

..............................................................................................................

..............................................................................................................

..............................................................................................................

..............................................................................................................

..............................................................................................................

# My review

First impressions

Review

What I liked
most about the book

..........................................................................................

..........................................................................................

..........................................................................................

..........................................................................................

..........................................................................................

..........................................................................................

What I disliked

..........................................................................................

..........................................................................................

..........................................................................................

..........................................................................................

..........................................................................................

..........................................................................................

*I am a part of everything
that I have read.*

Theodore Roosevelt

Other books in the same series

Other books by the same author

Other books with similar themes

Written by

Year of publication

Number of pages

Fiction Nonfiction

Genre

Date started Completed

| Characters | Plot | Writing | Overall rating |
| --- | --- | --- | --- |
| ☆☆☆☆☆ | ☆☆☆☆☆ | ☆☆☆☆☆ | ☆☆☆☆☆ |

How I discovered this book

What the book is about

Book summary

*The ability to read awoke inside of me some long dormant craving to be mentally alive.*

**Malcolm X**

Main characters

My favorite character was

Why I liked this character

Main themes

..........

Writing style

..........

Memorable quotes

..........

..........

..........

..........

..........

..........

..........

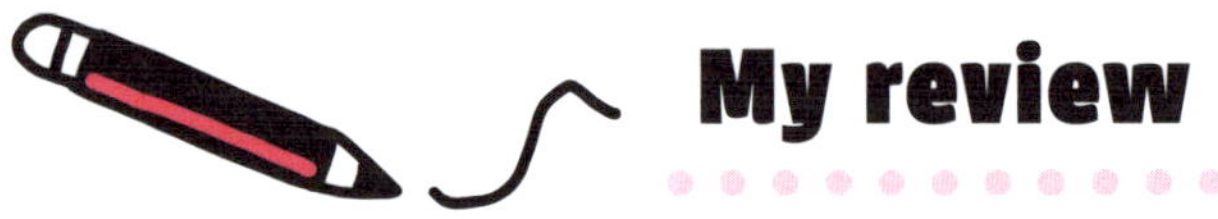

# My review

First impressions

Review

What I liked most about the book

..........................................................................................

..........................................................................................

..........................................................................................

..........................................................................................

..........................................................................................

..........................................................................................

What I disliked

..........................................................................................

..........................................................................................

..........................................................................................

..........................................................................................

..........................................................................................

..........................................................................................

*I love deadlines. I love the whooshing noise they make as they go by.*

**Douglas Adams**

Other books in the same series

Other books by the same author

Other books with similar themes

## BOOKS I'D LIKE TO READ

*I can shake off everything as I write; my sorrows disappear, my courage is reborn.*

Anne Frank

## BOOKS I HAVE READ AND REVIEWED

| PAGE | BOOK TITLE |
| --- | --- |
| | |
| | |
| | |
| | |
| | |
| | |
| | |
| | |
| | |
| | |
| | |
| | |
| | |
| | |
| | |

| PAGE | BOOK TITLE |
| --- | --- |
| | |
| | |
| | |
| | |
| | |
| | |
| | |
| | |
| | |
| | |
| | |
| | |
| | |
| | |
| | |

| PAGE | BOOK TITLE |
| --- | --- |
| | |
| | |
| | |
| | |
| | |
| | |
| | |
| | |
| | |
| | |
| | |
| | |
| | |
| | |
| | |
| | |